TMD

Too Much Drama
A Biblical Perspective

Dr. C. Dexter Wise III

Wise Works, Inc.
Westerville, Ohio

TMD

Too Much Drama:
A Biblical Perspective

Unless otherwise indicated, all scripture quotations are taken from the *New King James Version* of the Holy Bible.

Cover design by Earl L. Lee III.

TMD
Too Much Drama
A Biblical Perspective

ISBN: 978-0-9818828-6-4
Copyright © 2009 by C. Dexter Wise III

Published by Wise Works, Inc.
P.O. Box 0771
Westerville, Ohio 43086
Phone: (614) 898-1997
www.wiseworksonline.com

Printed in the United States of America. All rights reserved under International Copyright Law. Contents and/or cover may not be reproduced in whole or in part in any form without the express written consent of the publisher.

Too Much Drama:
A Biblical Perspective

Table of Contents

Preface, p. 6

Introduction, p. 8

1.
The Script
It Structures You – p. 11

2.
The Part
It was Destined for You – p. 17

3.
The Cast
It Influences You – p. 23

4.
The Director
He Guides You – p. 28

5.
The Agent
He Intercedes for You – p. 32

6.
The Money
It Tempts You – p. 37

TMD
Too Much Drama:
A Biblical Perspective

7.
The Location
It Lifts or Limits You – p. 41

8.
The Stage
It Elevates You – p. 46

9.
The Lighting
It Shows You – p. 53

10.
The Props
They Support You – p. 58

11.
The Music
It Encourages You – p. 62

12.
The Curtain
It Separates You – p. 66

13.
The Audience
It Watches You – p. 71

Too Much Drama:
A Biblical Perspective

14.
The Critics
They Focus You – p. 76

15.
The Applause
It Praises You – p. 82

16.
The Drama
It Blesses You – p. 85

17.
The Credits
They Helped You – p. 89

Too Much Drama:
A Biblical Perspective

Preface:

Too Much Drama: *A Biblical Perspective*

The book *Too Much Drama: What to Do When Your Life is Going Over the Top* has an implicit biblical foundation. Underlying every line of it is the conviction that, for the most part, the drama which we face and our ability to deal with it, is connected to our relationship with and trust in God. Still, that book was written using general and practical life experiences as the illustrations to make the argument. I hope you purchase a copy, read it and enjoy it on its own merits.

This present work, however, attempts to make the same case in a complimentary manner using explicit references to biblical people and passages. It is intended for: 1. personal Bible study and reflection; 2. small group meetings; and 3. as a resource for larger Christian growth study settings.

Too Much Drama: A Biblical Perspective constitutes the notes to the video teaching in which I personally take you through each of the lessons in this book. These Bible study outlines have been written to

stand alone without the video. Nevertheless, they

will make much, much more sense when coupled with the video.

What you are holding in your hand is the skeleton of the teaching. If you want the meat, the clothes, the make-up and all the accessories, you will have to watch the video along with it. When you do, each lesson will come alive.

Therefore, I encourage you to purchase a copy of the video for yourself and/or one for each of your small group leaders. This way, everyone can get the maximum benefit of what this curriculum has to offer.

Dr. C. Dexter Wise III
Westerville, Ohio
December 2009

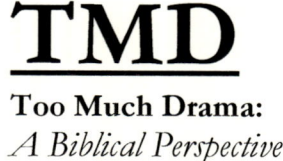

Too Much Drama:
A Biblical Perspective

Introduction:

Drama Points

Reflexology is the study and practice of foot and hand massage. According to Lucinda Lidell,

Reflexology is based on the principle that there are areas, or reflex points, on the feet and hands that correspond to each organ, gland and structure in the body. By working on these reflexes, the reflexologist reduces tension over all the body. (The Book of Massage: The Complete Step-by-Step Guide to Eastern and Western Techniques, p. 130)

In other words, if there is tension or pain in a certain part of the body, an expert reflexologist should be able to identify the spot on the hand or foot which is associated with it, massage that spot and thereby reduce or relieve the tension or pain experienced.

When some people study reflexology, they call it science. When others consider it, they call it pseudo-science. When still others hear about it, they call it psycho-somatic. However, whatever *you* may call it, all of us know that when our feet hurt, our whole body hurts! And when we get a good foot massage,

Too Much Drama:
A Biblical Perspective

we feel great all over. Thus, reflexology may not be as widely accepted as other therapeutic practices, but you have to admit, it seems like *there's something to it!*

In a similar way, the drama in your life is just like the reflex points on your hands and feet. There are certain types of drama which you experience that correspond to the various "drama producing aspects" of a production such as a play, a television show, a video or a movie. Hence, if you ever desire to increase, enhance, reduce or relieve the drama in your life, simply check the status of one or more of the "drama producing aspects" in it.

For the sake of our discussion, I am going to call these "drama producing aspects" *drama points*. These drama points are dimensions of the action in your life. They are the simple aspects which can make or break your story. Each one alone or in combination with others can be vital to the level, the length and the life of your drama.

Therefore, if you find yourself experiencing too much drama (or not enough drama for that matter), what follows in the rest of this book is a list of the likely places to check as major culprits of it. Since,

TMD
Too Much Drama:
A Biblical Perspective

therefore, each drama point produces its own unique type of drama, each deserves and will receive its own separate consideration.

You may call this approach science. You may call this analysis pseudo-science. You may call this exercise completely psychotic. Yet, once you see the connections based on this concept, I trust that you will agree – *there's something to it!*

Now that you have an understanding of what we're trying to achieve and the approach we intend to take, let's go right to the lesson on the first drama point – *The Script.*

Too Much Drama:
A Biblical Perspective

1.
The Script
It Structures You

The Passage: Jonah 1: 1-16

1 Now the word of the LORD came to Jonah the son of Amittai, saying, 2"Arise, go to Nineveh, that great city, and cry out against it; for their wickedness has come up before Me." 3But Jonah arose to flee to Tarshish from the presence of the LORD. He went down to Joppa, and found a ship going to Tarshish; so he paid the fare, and went down into it, to go with them to Tarshish from the presence of the LORD.

4 But the LORD sent out a great wind on the sea, and there was a mighty tempest on the sea, so that the ship was about to be broken up.

5Then the mariners were afraid; and every man cried out to his god, and threw the cargo that was in the ship into the sea, to lighten the load. But Jonah had gone down into the lowest parts of the ship, had lain down, and was fast asleep.

6So the captain came to him, and said to him, "What do you mean, sleeper? Arise, call on your God; perhaps your God will consider us, so that we may not perish."

TMD

Too Much Drama:
A Biblical Perspective

---

7 And they said to one another, "Come, let us cast lots, that we may know for whose cause this trouble has come upon us." So they cast lots, and the lot fell on Jonah. 8 Then they said to him, "Please tell us! For whose cause is this trouble upon us? What is your occupation? And where do you come from? What is your country? And of what people are you?"

9 So he said to them, "I am a Hebrew; and I fear the LORD, the God of heaven, who made the sea and the dry land."

10 Then the men were exceedingly afraid, and said to him, "Why have you done this?" For the men knew that he fled from the presence of the LORD, because he had told them. 11 Then they said to him, "What shall we do to you that the sea may be calm for us?"--for the sea was growing more tempestuous.
12 And he said to them, "Pick me up and throw me into the sea; then the sea will become calm for you. For I know that this great tempest is because of me."

13 Nevertheless the men rowed hard to return to land, but they could not, for the sea continued to grow more tempestuous against them. 14 Therefore they cried out to the LORD and said, "We pray, O LORD, please do not let us perish for this man's life, and do not charge us with innocent blood; for You, O LORD, have done as it pleased You." 15 So they picked up Jonah and threw him into the sea, and the sea ceased from its raging. 16 Then the men feared the LORD exceedingly, and offered a sacrifice to the LORD and took vows.

Too Much Drama:
A Biblical Perspective

The Person: Jonah

Talk about too much drama! The book of Jonah is one of the smallest books in the Bible. Yet, there are few books which have more drama in it. This is primarily because its principle character is a prophet who is himself full of drama.

The book opens with a simple command of God to Jonah. God orders Jonah to go to a city called Nineveh and tell them to repent or else He will destroy them and their city. Nineveh was the capital of Assyria which was, by the way, a major adversary of Israel. Jonah knew that if he preached repentance to Nineveh, they would turn from their sin and God would turn from His wrath towards them.

Therefore, since he did not want his enemy saved, instead of going to Nineveh as commanded, he bought a ticket on a ship which was headed in the other direction to a city called Tarshish.

It is at this point that, after only the first three verses of the book, the serious drama begins! All of it was because Jonah decided not to stick to God's script.

TMD

Too Much Drama:
A Biblical Perspective

The Points:

Observe the following points on the importance of following God's script:

1. Your script is not simply the lines you write for yourself. It is the set of instructions God gives to you for your life. (Jonah 1: 1-2)

2. You always have an option whether or not to follow your God given script. (Jonah 1: 3)

3. Failure to follow your God given script almost always leads you and those around you into a great storm. (Jonah 1: 4)

4. The winds in your life will stop blowing and the whales in your life will stop swallowing when you decide to go back to the script. (Jonah 1: 14-15)

5. Your disobedience to or deviation from the script does not change the script. (Jonah 3: 1-3)

Too Much Drama:
A Biblical Perspective

The Practice:

Here is how you can put this passage into practice.

1. Find out God's script for you through reading the Holy Scriptures.

2. Find out God's script for you through prayer and fasting.

3. Follow God's script for you with the help of the Holy Spirit.

The Ponderings:

1. Do you have a general or specific sense of what God's script for your life is?

2. How much flexibility do you think God gives us to "interpret" as we follow His script?

3. Have you ever deviated from what you knew to be God's script for you? What happened?

TMD
Too Much Drama:
A Biblical Perspective

4. Have you ever followed God's script in a specific situation? What happened?

Too Much Drama:
A Biblical Perspective

2.
The Part
It was Destined for You

The Passage: Esther 4: 1-17

1 When Mordecai learned all that had happened, he tore his clothes and put on sackcloth and ashes, and went out into the midst of the city. He cried out with a loud and bitter cry. 2He went as far as the front of the king's gate, for no one might enter the king's gate clothed with sackcloth. 3And in every province where the king's command and decree arrived, there was great mourning among the Jews, with fasting, weeping, and wailing; and many lay in sackcloth and ashes.

4So Esther's maids and eunuchs came and told her, and the queen was deeply distressed. Then she sent garments to clothe Mordecai and take his sackcloth away from him, but he would not accept them. 5Then Esther called Hathach, one of the king's eunuchs whom he had appointed to attend her, and she gave him a command concerning Mordecai, to learn what and why this was. 6So Hathach went out to Mordecai in the city square that was in front of the king's gate. 7And Mordecai told him all that had happened to him, and the sum of money that Haman had promised to pay into the king's treasuries to destroy the Jews. 8He also gave him a copy of the written decree for their destruction, which was

TMD
Too Much Drama:
A Biblical Perspective

---

given at Shushan, that he might show it to Esther and explain it to her, and that he might command her to go in to the king to make supplication to him and plead before him for her people. 9So Hathach returned and told Esther the words of Mordecai.

10Then Esther spoke to Hathach, and gave him a command for Mordecai: 11"All the king's servants and the people of the king's provinces know that any man or woman who goes into the inner court to the king, who has not been called, he has but one law: put all to death, except the one to whom the king holds out the golden scepter, that he may live. Yet I myself have not been called to go in to the king these thirty days." 12So they told Mordecai Esther's words.

13And Mordecai told them to answer Esther: "Do not think in your heart that you will escape in the king's palace any more than all the other Jews. 14For if you remain completely silent at this time, relief and deliverance will arise for the Jews from another place, but you and your father's house will perish. Yet who knows whether you have come to the kingdom for such a time as this?"

15Then Esther told them to reply to Mordecai: 16"Go, gather all the Jews who are present in Shushan, and fast for me; neither eat nor drink for three days, night or day. My maids and I will fast likewise. And so I will go to the king, which is against the law; and if I perish, I perish!"

17So Mordecai went his way and did according to all that Esther

Too Much Drama:
A Biblical Perspective

commanded him.

The Person: Esther

Esther began life at a disadvantage. Her parents died while she was still a child. Consequently, she was adopted and raised by her uncle Mordecai as his own daughter. Being a Jewish girl in a Persian kingdom, Esther had no real expectation or aspiration of ever becoming anything other than an average wife and mother.

A major opening occurred for her when Queen Vashti was dethroned by King Ahasuerus for what he thought was her *disrespectful* behavior towards him. Soon after this, a beauty contest was held to find the most beautiful woman in the kingdom to replace Vashti.

At the urging of her uncle, Esther entered the contest and a year later was chosen by the king to be his queen. You would think that this fairy tale drama might conclude here with a happy ending. However, this is where the plot thickens and the real drama actually begins.

TMD

Too Much Drama:
A Biblical Perspective

One of the king's advisors by the name of Haman is irrationally irritated by Esther's uncle, Mordecai. Consequently, he convinces King Ahasuerus to kill all of the Jews in his kingdom on a certain day. The king does not know that his wife Esther is also a Jew.

So, when the news of Haman's plot reaches Mordecai, he sends a message to Esther. In it, he tells her that she must speak to the king in order to prevent the slaughter of her people.

At first, Esther is reluctant. However, she finally comes to the realization that she has a part to play and that, even if it costs her life, she must play it.

The Points:

Consider these points on Esther's part.

1. Esther thought she was being groomed to play one part when, in fact, she was being put in position to play another. (Esther 2: 8-18)

2. Esther was meant to play her part, but if she had refused to do so, another person would

Too Much Drama:
A Biblical Perspective

have taken her place. (Esther 4: 13)

3. Esther only had a limited time to play her part. (Esther 4: 14)

4. Esther accepted her role and covered it with prayer. (Esther 4: 16)

5. Esther took a risk to play her part. (Esther 4: 16)

6. Esther played her part with wisdom. (Esther 5: 1-8; 7: 1-4)

7. Esther's role seemed minor, but it saved a nation. (Esther 8: 1-17)

The Practice:

Here is how you can put this passage into practice.

1. You must know and understand your part.

2. You must be in position to play your part.

TMD
Too Much Drama:
A Biblical Perspective

3. You must seek God's guidance to play your part.

4. You must have courage and faith to play your part.

5. You must remember you have a *part* and not the *whole*.

The Ponderings:

1. What part are you called to play in the body of Christ?

2. Have you ever encountered trouble when you tried to play the wrong part? Explain.

3. How can believers play their parts for the Lord without being guilty of "acting?"

4. Why does it require courage and faith to play your part?

Too Much Drama:
A Biblical Perspective

3.
The Cast
It Influences You

The Passage: Luke 6: 12-16

12Now it came to pass in those days that He went out to the mountain to pray, and continued all night in prayer to God. 13And when it was day, He called His disciples to Himself; and from them He chose twelve whom He also named apostles:

14Simon, whom He also named Peter, and Andrew his brother; James and John; Philip and Bartholomew; 15Matthew and Thomas; James the son of Alphaeus, and Simon called the Zealot; 16Judas the son of James, and Judas Iscariot who also became a traitor.

The Person: Jesus

The great drama of salvation had already been initiated. Jesus had already been born. He had already been dedicated in the temple. He had already been raised to the age of maturity. He had already been baptized by John in the Jordan. He had already been tempted by Satan in the wilderness.

Too Much Drama:
A Biblical Perspective

Now, as he embarked upon his public ministry, even the Son of God realized that He could not do it alone.

Hence, according to this text, Jesus prayed all night before choosing the twelve men who would closely walk and talk with Him for three years as His disciples.

As the gospel story unfolds from this point, it becomes clearer and clearer that each of the characters in the cast which Jesus chose to help His cause brought their own unique gifts, quirks and drama with them.

As it was with Jesus, so it is with us. When we chose the people who will share our lives, we also, to some extent, chose the drama of our lives.

The Points:

The twelve disciples were men chosen by Jesus. They were not merely drawn to Him. He was drawn to them. What, then, could it possibly be about each of them that Jesus saw in them? Furthermore, what

Too Much Drama:
A Biblical Perspective

does His choosing them tell us about the type of characters we should have in our *supporting* cast?

Consider this:

1. *Simon Peter* – Someone who may not be right all the time, but is raw and real all the time. (Mark 14: 28-31)

2. *Andrew* – Someone who is constantly bringing others into your life to advance your cause. (John 1: 40-42)

3. *James* – Someone who wants to be at the top. (Mark 10: 35-37)

4. *John* – Someone you can count on to be there for you no matter what. (John 19: 25-27)

5. *Philip* – Someone who brings diversity to your life. (Philip brought the Greeks to see Jesus.) (John 12: 20-22)

6. *Bartholomew* (Nathaniel) – Someone who loves you even though they know where you came from. (John 1: 43-51)

TMD
Too Much Drama:
A Biblical Perspective

---

7. *Matthew* – Someone who understands how the world works including its darker side. (Matthew 9: 9)

8. *Thomas* – Someone who may doubt at first, but once convinced will go with you even unto death. (John 11: 7-16)

9. *James* – Someone who is youthful and thereby keeps you current and fresh. (Mark 15: 40)

10. *Simon the Zealot* – Someone with a passion about changing the injustices in the way things are. (Luke 6: 15)

11. *Judas the son of James.* – Someone who cannot be judged by their name. (Luke 6: 15)

12. *Judas Iscariot* – Someone who pushes you towards your purpose even if by means of an unpleasant method. (Matthew 26: 24-25)

The Practice:

Here is how you can put this passage into practice.

Too Much Drama:
A Biblical Perspective

1. All of us have a cast around us. The question is: *"What are the consequences which accompany those chosen by us?"*

2. A good drama requires diverse characters and so does life.

3. The cast we choose should help us complete the destiny for which we have been chosen.

The Ponderings:

1. Why is choosing the right cast so important to the drama in your life?

2. How are we to determine and manage the cast of characters in our life? Can this even be done?

3. Why do you think that Jesus included a man like Judas in His cast?

4. What does your cast have to do with your purpose in life?

Too Much Drama:
A Biblical Perspective

4.
The Director
He Guides You

The Passage: Proverbs 3: 5-6

5Trust in the LORD with all your heart, And lean not on your own understanding; 6In all your ways acknowledge Him, And He shall direct your paths.

The Person: Solomon

King Solomon was the fruit of drama. Before he was born, his father, King David, and his mother, Bathsheba, conceived a child through an adulterous relationship. That episode ended in the death of Bathsheba's husband, Uriah, and the death of the child they had conceived. Once David and Bathsheba were "properly married," they gave birth to Solomon.

This king's son not only grew up in the middle of his father's drama, but being the wealthiest man on the planet with 700 wives and 300 concubines *and* two

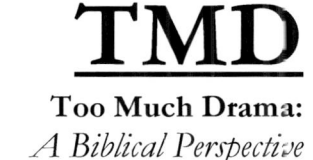

Too Much Drama:
A Biblical Perspective

hot headed rebellious sons, he had enough drama of his own!

In the *Book of Proverbs*, which is attributed to him, it seems as if he is trying to teach his son all the things he needs to know to avoid having too much drama in his life. At the core of this advice is for the young man to allow the Lord to direct his paths. In other words, Solomon is saying: *"No matter how high you may rise or how much you may have, if you expect your drama to have a positive outcome, then, listen to your director."*

The Points:

Even though the script may have been clearly written, it is the director who assists the actor in properly performing it. This is why you should:

1. Trust your director because He is the Lord. (Proverbs 3: 5)

2. Trust your director with all your heart. (Proverbs 3: 5)

3. Trust your director even when you do not

Too Much Drama:
A Biblical Perspective

understand. (Proverbs 3: 5)

4. Trust your director through your actions. (Proverbs 3: 6)

5. Trust your director enough to acknowledge Him. (Proverbs 3: 6)

6. Trust your director to direct your paths. (Proverbs 3: 6)

The Practice:

Here is how you can put this passage into practice.

1. Seek your director's opinion.

2. Accept your director's correction.

3. Follow your director's instructions.

The Ponderings:

1. Why is it often difficult for believers to trust

TMD

Too Much Drama:
A Biblical Perspective

2. in the Lord?

3. Why are we so prone to lean towards our own understanding?

4. What does it mean to acknowledge the Lord in all your ways?

5. Has the Lord ever directed your path? Elaborate.

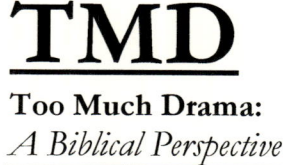

Too Much Drama:
A Biblical Perspective

5.
The Agent
He Intercedes for You

The Passage: Exodus 2: 1-10

1 And a man of the house of Levi went and took as wife a daughter of Levi. 2So the woman conceived and bore a son. And when she saw that he was a beautiful child, she hid him three months. 3But when she could no longer hide him, she took an ark of bulrushes for him, daubed it with asphalt and pitch, put the child in it, and laid it in the reeds by the river's bank. 4And his sister stood afar off, to know what would be done to him.

5Then the daughter of Pharaoh came down to bathe at the river. And her maidens walked along the riverside; and when she saw the ark among the reeds, she sent her maid to get it. 6And when she opened it, she saw the child, and behold, the baby wept. So she had compassion on him, and said, "This is one of the Hebrews' children."

7Then his sister said to Pharaoh's daughter, "Shall I go and call a nurse for you from the Hebrew women, that she may nurse the child for you?"

8And Pharaoh's daughter said to her, "Go." So the maiden went and called the child's mother. 9Then Pharaoh's daughter said to

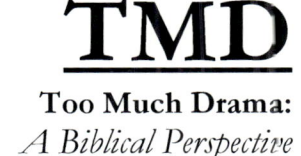

Too Much Drama:
A Biblical Perspective

her, "Take this child away and nurse him for me, and I will give you your wages." So the woman took the child and nursed him.

10 And the child grew, and she brought him to Pharaoh's daughter, and he became her son. So she called his name Moses, saying, "Because I drew him out of the water."

The Person: Miriam

For centuries, we have sung the praises of a man named Moses. It was Moses who confronted Pharaoh with the word of God: *"Let My people go!"* It was Moses who presided over the ten plagues of Egypt. It was Moses who stood before the Red Sea until it parted. It was Moses for whom God rained down bread from heaven and spouted water out of a rock. It was Moses who received the Ten Commandments on Mt. Sinai after speaking with God face to face. It was Moses who led Israel out of bondage and put her on the way to the Promised Land.

However, with all the praise that we heap upon the man Moses, the passage before us now reminds us that had it not been for a little girl named Miriam, we

Too Much Drama:
A Biblical Perspective

may have never heard of Moses. Miriam was the big sister of Moses whose quick thinking and courageous intercession saved his life as a little child. Her intercessory actions teach us that many times the reason that we get to play great parts in the dramas of life has little to do with our talent, skill or even worthiness. More often than not, it is because we have a great agent working behind the scenes on our behalf.

The Points:

In the title of this lesson, it refers to the agent as "he," but in this case, the agent is a "she." Here are some points you should not miss.

1. Notice all of the intercessors it took to keep Moses from being killed as a baby:

    a. His mother, Jocebed, who disobeyed Pharaoh's command to kill all of the newborn Hebrew baby boys. (Exodus 2: 1-2)

    b. Pharaoh's daughter who drew him out of

TMD
Too Much Drama:
A Biblical Perspective

the river. (Exodus 2: 5-6)

    c. His sister, Miriam who interceded for him. (Exodus 2: 7)

2. Intercessors like Miriam see the need. (Exodus 2: 4)

3. Intercessors like Miriam step into the situation. (Exodus 2: 7)

4. Intercessors like Miriam speak up on behalf of others. (Exodus 2: 8)

5. Intercessors like Miriam come out with a win, win solution. (Exodus 2: 8)

The Practice:

Here is how you can put this passage into practice.

1. Pray for God to send godly intercessors into your life.

2. Be an intercessor for others.

TMD
Too Much Drama:
A Biblical Perspective

3. Rely on the Holy Spirit to intercede with the Father for you.

The Ponderings:

1. Give an example of someone who interceded for you.

2. Give an example of someone you interceded for.

3. Give an example of how Christ has interceded for you in the past and does intercede for you right now.

Too Much Drama:
A Biblical Perspective

6.
The Money
It Tempts You

The Passage: Matthew 26: 14-16

14 Then one of the twelve, called Judas Iscariot, went to the chief priests 15and said, "What are you willing to give me if I deliver Him to you?" And they counted out to him thirty pieces of silver. 16So from that time he sought opportunity to betray Him.

The Person: Judas

Judas Iscariot is named in every list of Jesus' twelve disciples. However, even though he may have been *among* the twelve disciples, virtually any Bible reader can get the sense that he was hardly *one* of the twelve disciples.

The term *Iscariot*, which often follows his name, is not really his name. The word literally means *"man from Kerioth."* It refers to the region from which he came. He was, therefore, the only one of the twelve who did not come from Galilee. Based on this,

Too Much Drama:
A Biblical Perspective

perhaps, even he felt that he was not one of them. We know from this scripture and others that Judas

betrayed Jesus. What shocks us is that it was not for philosophical reasons. As far as we know, it was not for a difference in theology. No one believes that it was because Jesus had mistreated him and by betraying the Lord, he was seeking revenge. *The hurtful and hard truth is that Judas did it all for the money.*

It is amazing how often money is the motive behind drama and what some people are willing to sell to get it.

The Points:

From the drama of Judas we learn:

1. Money can make you insensitive to the needs of others. (John 12: 3-6)

2. Money can tempt you to steal. (John 12: 6)

3. Money can entice you to do anything for it. (Matthew 26: 15)

Too Much Drama:
A Biblical Perspective

4. Money can have you act hypocritically. (Matthew 26: 25)

5. Money can make you betray someone you love and who loves you. (Matthew 26: 47-50)

6. Money can make you try to *pay* for your sins. (Matthew 27: 3-4)

7. Money can make you sorry that you made it your master. (Matthew 27: 5)

The Practice:

Here is how you can put this passage into practice.

1. Whenever money is involved, be sure to carefully examine your motives.

2. Money was not made to master you. You were made to master your money.

3. Too much drama is a sure thing whenever the love of money is directing the action.

TMD
Too Much Drama:
A Biblical Perspective

The Ponderings:

1. Why do you think that money and drama are so closely associated with each other?

2. What do you think it means to master your money?

3. How does money deceive and betray people?

4. How can the lack of money or the abundance of money be a problem?

Too Much Drama:
A Biblical Perspective

7.
The Location
It Lifts or Limits You

The Passage: Genesis 13: 1-13

1 Then Abram went up from Egypt, he and his wife and all that he had, and Lot with him, to the South. 2 Abram was very rich in livestock, in silver, and in gold. 3 And he went on his journey from the South as far as Bethel, to the place where his tent had been at the beginning, between Bethel and Ai, 4 to the place of the altar which he had made there at first. And there Abram called on the name of the LORD.

5 Lot also, who went with Abram, had flocks and herds and tents. 6 Now the land was not able to support them, that they might dwell together, for their possessions were so great that they could not dwell together. 7 And there was strife between the herdsmen of Abram's livestock and the herdsmen of Lot's livestock. The Canaanites and the Perizzites then dwelt in the land.

8 So Abram said to Lot, "Please let there be no strife between you and me, and between my herdsmen and your herdsmen; for we are brethren. 9 Is not the whole land before you? Please separate from me. If you take the left, then I will go to the right; or, if you go to the right, then I will go to the left."

TMD

Too Much Drama:
A Biblical Perspective

10And Lot lifted his eyes and saw all the plain of Jordan, that it was well watered everywhere (before the LORD destroyed Sodom and Gomorrah) like the garden of the LORD, like the land of Egypt as you go toward Zoar. 11Then Lot chose for himself all the plain of Jordan, and Lot journeyed east. And they separated from each other. 12Abram dwelt in the land of Canaan, and Lot dwelt in the cities of the plain and pitched his tent even as far as Sodom. 13But the men of Sodom were exceedingly wicked and sinful against the LORD.

The Person: Lot

When Abraham left the city of Ur looking for the land of promise, his nephew Lot went with him. Even before Abraham ever entered the Promised Land, he began to receive God's promised prosperity. Since Lot was with Abraham, he prospered too.

In fact, they both prospered so much that the land in which they dwelt could not bear them together. Their herdsmen began to be at odds over space and livestock, so, Abraham gave Lot a choice. He said in essence: *"Let's not fight about this. If you go to the left, I will go to the right. If you go the right, I will go to the left."*

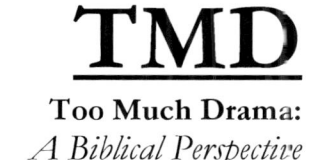

Too Much Drama:
A Biblical Perspective

The Bible says that Lot lifted up his eyes and saw the land of Sodom and Gomorrah. It was *"well watered like the garden of the Lord."* Thus, Lot headed for Sodom and Gomorrah. When he arrived there, he quickly discovered that what real estate agents say about real estate is also true about drama, it's all about *location, location, location!*

The Points:

Learn these lessons from Lot's location.

1. Lot's location with Abraham led to his prosperity. (Genesis 13: 5)

2. Lot's location with Abraham also led to strife. (Genesis 13: 6-7)

3. Lot's location was his own choice. (Genesis 13: 8-9; 11)

4. Lot's location in Sodom and Gomorrah was based primarily on the looks of the land. (Genesis 13: 10)

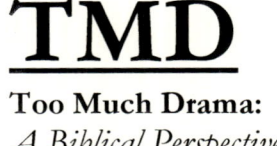

Too Much Drama:
A Biblical Perspective

---

5. Lot's location was one of wickedness and sin. (Genesis 13: 13)

6. Lot's location was not compatible with the values of a righteous man. (Genesis 13: 13)

7. Lot's location in Sodom and Gomorrah was not his last location. Once God delivers you from such a godless place, you should move forward and never look back. (Genesis 19: 15-17)

The Practice:

Here is how you can put this passage into practice.

1. There is more to a land than its looks.

2. When you choose your location, you also choose your experience.

3. God will be with you wherever you go.

Too Much Drama:
A Biblical Perspective

The Ponderings:

1. Give an example of how you experienced a change when you changed locations.

2. What can godly people do to survive in an ungodly location until they are able to leave or be delivered from it?

3. Is location only a matter of a physical place or can we also be challenged because of our "location" in other areas as well? Explain.

4. How can being "in Christ" help us with the location issues we face?

Too Much Drama:
A Biblical Perspective

8.
The Stage
It Elevates You

The Passage: I Samuel 17: 12-47

12Now David was the son of that Ephrathite of Bethlehem Judah, whose name was Jesse, and who had eight sons. And the man was old, advanced in years, in the days of Saul. 13The three oldest sons of Jesse had gone to follow Saul to the battle. The names of his three sons who went to the battle were Eliab the firstborn, next to him Abinadab, and the third Shammah. 14David was the youngest. And the three oldest followed Saul. 15But David occasionally went and returned from Saul to feed his father's sheep at Bethlehem. 16And the Philistine drew near and presented himself forty days, morning and evening.

17Then Jesse said to his son David, "Take now for your brothers an ephah of this dried grain and these ten loaves, and run to your brothers at the camp. 18And carry these ten cheeses to the captain of their thousand, and see how your brothers fare, and bring back news of them." 19Now Saul and they and all the men of Israel were in the Valley of Elah, fighting with the Philistines.

20So David rose early in the morning, left the sheep with a keeper, and took the things and went as Jesse had commanded him. And he came to the camp as the army was going out to the fight and

TMD

Too Much Drama:
A Biblical Perspective

shouting for the battle. 21For Israel and the Philistines had drawn up in battle array, army against army. 22And David left his supplies in the hand of the supply keeper, ran to the army, and came and greeted his brothers. 23Then as he talked with them, there was the champion, the Philistine of Gath, Goliath by name, coming up from the armies of the Philistines; and he spoke according to the same words. So David heard them. 24And all the men of Israel, when they saw the man, fled from him and were dreadfully afraid. 25So the men of Israel said, "Have you seen this man who has come up? Surely he has come up to defy Israel; and it shall be that the man who kills him the king will enrich with great riches, will give him his daughter, and give his father's house exemption from taxes in Israel."

26Then David spoke to the men who stood by him, saying, "What shall be done for the man who kills this Philistine and takes away the reproach from Israel? For who is this uncircumcised Philistine, that he should defy the armies of the living God?"

27And the people answered him in this manner, saying, "So shall it be done for the man who kills him."
28Now Eliab his oldest brother heard when he spoke to the men; and Eliab's anger was aroused against David, and he said, "Why did you come down here? And with whom have you left those few sheep in the wilderness? I know your pride and the insolence of your heart, for you have come down to see the battle."

29And David said, "What have I done now? Is there not a

TMD
Too Much Drama:
A Biblical Perspective

---

cause?" 30Then he turned from him toward another and said the same thing; and these people answered him as the first ones did. 31Now when the words which David spoke were heard, they reported them to Saul; and he sent for him. 32Then David said to Saul, "Let no man's heart fail because of him; your servant will go and fight with this Philistine."

33And Saul said to David, "You are not able to go against this Philistine to fight with him; for you are a youth, and he a man of war from his youth."

34But David said to Saul, "Your servant used to keep his father's sheep, and when a lion or a bear came and took a lamb out of the flock, 35I went out after it and struck it, and delivered the lamb from its mouth; and when it arose against me, I caught it by its beard, and struck and killed it. 36Your servant has killed both lion and bear; and this uncircumcised Philistine will be like one of them, seeing he has defied the armies of the living God." 37Moreover David said, "The LORD, who delivered me from the paw of the lion and from the paw of the bear, He will deliver me from the hand of this Philistine."

And Saul said to David, "Go, and the LORD be with you!"

38So Saul clothed David with his armor, and he put a bronze helmet on his head; he also clothed him with a coat of mail. 39David fastened his sword to his armor and tried to walk, for he had not tested them. And David said to Saul, "I cannot walk

TMD
Too Much Drama:
A Biblical Perspective

with these, for I have not tested them." So David took them off. 40Then he took his staff in his hand; and he chose for himself five smooth stones from the brook, and put them in a shepherd's bag, in a pouch which he had, and his sling was in his hand. And he drew near to the Philistine. 41So the Philistine came, and began drawing near to David, and the man who bore the shield went before him. 42And when the Philistine looked about and saw David, he disdained him; for he was only a youth, ruddy and good-looking. 43So the Philistine said to David, "Am I a dog, that you come to me with sticks?" And the Philistine cursed David by his gods. 44And the Philistine said to David, "Come to me, and I will give your flesh to the birds of the air and the beasts of the field!"

45Then David said to the Philistine, "You come to me with a sword, with a spear, and with a javelin. But I come to you in the name of the LORD of hosts, the God of the armies of Israel, whom you have defied. 46This day the LORD will deliver you into my hand, and I will strike you and take your head from you. And this day I will give the carcasses of the camp of the Philistines to the birds of the air and the wild beasts of the earth, that all the earth may know that there is a God in Israel. 47Then all this assembly shall know that the LORD does not save with sword and spear; for the battle is the LORD's, and He will give you into our hands."

TMD

Too Much Drama:
A Biblical Perspective

The Person: David

David's brothers were right. He was an ambitious actor looking for a stage on which to perform. He got his first big break when his father, Jesse, sent him to the battle front to bring food to his older brothers.

While he was there, he happened to hear Goliath, the champion of the Philistines, defy both the army and the God of Israel. This young shepherd took full advantage of the situation and walked right into the middle of the fray. And, as you probably already know, the rest is history!

In this lesson, we come to know that *the stage* is the public arena where we are privileged or pressured to show who we are, what we are made of and what we can do. Some stages have a greater history than others. Some stages have a larger audience than others. Some stages have more prestige than others. However, all stages offer those who would dare to stand upon them the opportunity to be seen and celebrated.

Too Much Drama:
A Biblical Perspective

The Points:

David lived a highly "staged" life. Notice:

1. David was offstage tending sheep when the prophet Samuel visited his father's house. (I Samuel 16: 11-13)

2. David was backstage at the battle waiting for his cue to emerge. (I Samuel 17: 20-23)

3. David was upstage at the battlefield as he "upstaged" his brothers and the other soldiers there with his courage. (I Samuel 17: 25-30)

4. David was on stage when he went to meet Goliath in the valley. (I Samuel 17: 40-50)

5. David was center stage when he slew Goliath and won the praise of Israel. (I Samuel 17: 55-58)

The Practice:

Here is how you can put this passage into practice.

TMD

Too Much Drama:
A Biblical Perspective

1. Be ready for the stage.

2. Be grateful for the stage.

3. Be confident on the stage.

The Ponderings:

1. Describe an opportunity you had to *literally* or *figuratively* be "on stage." What happened?

2. What are some of the *pros* and *cons* of being on stage?

3. Does a person ever really get off stage? Explain.

4. What are some of the common stages upon which most people experience drama?

Too Much Drama:
A Biblical Perspective

9.
The Lighting
It Shows You

The Passage: Genesis 29: 15-30

15 Then Laban said to Jacob, "Because you are my relative, should you therefore serve me for nothing? Tell me, what should your wages be?" 16Now Laban had two daughters: the name of the elder was Leah, and the name of the younger was Rachel. 17Leah's eyes were delicate, but Rachel was beautiful of form and appearance.

18Now Jacob loved Rachel; so he said, "I will serve you seven years for Rachel your younger daughter." 19And Laban said, "It is better that I give her to you than that I should give her to another man. Stay with me." 20So Jacob served seven years for Rachel, and they seemed only a few days to him because of the love he had for her.

21Then Jacob said to Laban, "Give me my wife, for my days are fulfilled, that I may go in to her." 22And Laban gathered together all the men of the place and made a feast. 23Now it came to pass in the evening, that he took Leah his daughter and brought her to Jacob; and he went in to her. 24And Laban gave his maid Zilpah to his daughter Leah as a maid. 25So it came to pass in the

TMD

Too Much Drama:
A Biblical Perspective

morning, that behold, it was Leah. And he said to Laban, "What is this you have done to me? Was it not for Rachel that I served you? Why then have you deceived me?"

26And Laban said, "It must not be done so in our country, to give the younger before the firstborn. 27Fulfill her week, and we will give you this one also for the service which you will serve with me still another seven years."

28Then Jacob did so and fulfilled her week. So he gave him his daughter Rachel as wife also. 29And Laban gave his maid Bilhah to his daughter Rachel as a maid. 30Then Jacob also went in to Rachel, and he also loved Rachel more than Leah. And he served with Laban still another seven years.

The Person: Jacob

Jacob was the grandson of Abraham and is always listed among the primary patriarchs of Israel - *Abraham, Isaac and Jacob!* He earned his name which means *supplanter* since throughout his life he more than once tried to get ahead of his twin brother Esau. He held onto Esau's heel coming out of the womb and he stole his birth right when they both became of age.

TMD
Too Much Drama:
A Biblical Perspective

The incident related in this passage involves Jacob, love, Laban and light. After he stole his brother's birth right, Jacob fled to his mother's country where he was received into the household of her brother Laban. Laban had a daughter named Rachel whom Jacob loved. He agreed to work seven years with Laban for the right to marry her.

When it came time for Jacob to marry Rachel, during the night of the wedding, Jacob went into the tent of a woman who he thought was Rachel. However, since he never bothered to *turn on the light* and check, he found out in the morning that it was her older sister Leah instead.

Jacob's uncle Laban had tricked him into having to work another seven years to earn Rachel's hand in marriage out right. In hindsight, Jacob would confess that all of this extra drama could have been avoided if he simply had the benefit of proper lighting.

The Points:

See the light we get from watching Jacob in the dark.

TMD

Too Much Drama:
A Biblical Perspective

---

1. Jacob, the trickster, was finally tricked.

   (Genesis 29: 23-26)

2. Jacob assumed that he did not need any light.
   (Genesis 29: 23)

3. Jacob was deceived because he did not have the advantage of the light. (Genesis 29: 23)

4. Jacob could have saved himself seven years of labor by simply getting some light.
   (Genesis 29: 26-30)

5. Jacob found out that what is done in the dark is eventually brought to light. (Genesis 29: 25)

6. Jacob learned that what is done in the dark may be exposed by the light, but it cannot be undone by the light. (Genesis 29: 26-30)

The Practice:

Here is how you can put this passage into practice.

TMD

Too Much Drama:
A Biblical Perspective

1. Never make major decisions in the dark.

2. Never enter into a serious relationship with people who you cannot clearly see.

3. Never wallow in the darkness. *Walk in the light.*

The Ponderings:

1. Why do you think darkness is attractive to so many people?

2. What types of things become clearly visible when they are seen in the light?

3. Describe an experience you had "in the dark" which might have turned out better had you used proper lighting.

4. What do you think it means to walk in the light?

TMD

Too Much Drama:
A Biblical Perspective

10.
The Props
They Support You

The Passage: Exodus 4: 10-17

10Then Moses said to the LORD, "O my Lord, I am not eloquent, neither before nor since You have spoken to Your servant; but I am slow of speech and slow of tongue."

11So the LORD said to him, "Who has made man's mouth? Or who makes the mute, the deaf, the seeing, or the blind? Have not I, the LORD? 12Now therefore, go, and I will be with your mouth and teach you what you shall say."

13But he said, "O my Lord, please send by the hand of whomever else You may send."

14So the anger of the LORD was kindled against Moses, and He said: "Is not Aaron the Levite your brother? I know that he can speak well. And look, he is also coming out to meet you. When he sees you, he will be glad in his heart. 15Now you shall speak to him and put the words in his mouth. And I will be with your mouth and with his mouth, and I will teach you what you shall do. 16So he shall be your spokesman to the people. And he himself shall be as a mouth for you, and you shall be to him as God. 17And you shall take this rod in your hand, with which you shall

do the signs."

The Person: Moses

Thanks to Hollywood's Cecil B. De Mills, the image that most of us have of Moses is one of a self-reliant mighty man. He is one who defies Pharaohs, performs miracles and walks through seas on dry land.

Actually, Moses was a stammering, stumbling and insecure leader who had to be dragged into the leadership of Israel's deliverance from Egypt. He was only able to do what he did with the help of human and inanimate props. God made sure that before Moses left the land of Midian, he was well equipped with props to ensure the completion of his task.

We too will discover that we need props along the way to help us fulfill our purpose. These props enhance the drama in our life. For without them, the drama might not be as real or might not happen at all.

TMD

Too Much Drama:
A Biblical Perspective

The Points:

Observe these points about the prophet Moses' props:

1. God gave Moses props because he complained about being inadequate. (Exodus 4: 10)

2. God gave Moses His presence as a prop to stand upon. (Exodus 4: 12)

3. God gave Moses, Aaron as a prop to speak for him. (Exodus 4: 14-15)

4. God gave Moses a rod as a prop to do miracles with. (Exodus 4: 17)

The Practice:

Here is how you can put this passage into practice.

1. Whenever God calls us to a task, He also provides us with the props to do it.

Too Much Drama:
A Biblical Perspective

2. Props cannot act alone. They must be used in faith by people.

3. Props are like training wheels on a bicycle. Do not be ashamed if you have to use them. That is why they are there – *to prop you up!*

The Ponderings:

1. How can having people in your life as props be good and bad?

2. What "props" has God placed in your life to help you fulfill His purpose for you? Elaborate.

3. How can props lead to dependence?

4. How can props lead to confidence?

Too Much Drama:
A Biblical Perspective

11.
The Music
It Encourages You

The Passage: Ephesians 5: 18-21; Acts 16: 25-26; Colossians 3: 16-17

Ephesians 5: 18-21

18 And do not be drunk with wine, in which is dissipation; but be filled with the Spirit, 19 speaking to one another in psalms and hymns and spiritual songs, singing and making melody in your heart to the Lord, 20 giving thanks always for all things to God the Father in the name of our Lord Jesus Christ, 21 submitting to one another in the fear of God.

Acts 16: 25

25 But at midnight Paul and Silas were praying and singing hymns to God, and the prisoners were listening to them. 26 Suddenly there was a great earthquake, so that the foundations of the prison were shaken; and immediately all the doors were opened and everyone's chains were loosed.

Too Much Drama:
A Biblical Perspective

Colossians 3: 16

16Let the word of Christ dwell in you richly in all wisdom, teaching and admonishing one another in psalms and hymns and spiritual songs, singing with grace in your hearts to the Lord.

17And whatever you do in word or deed, do all in the name of the Lord Jesus, giving thanks to God the Father through Him.

The Person: Paul

Maybe it's just me, but I never got the impression that Apostle Paul had the voice to do the lead in a gospel choir! With all the talk about his sicknesses and infirmities, while it could very well be possible, I personally don't see Paul as a soloist.

Yet, the record is quite clear that whether or not he was qualified to be a soloist, he was a singer. He sang regularly. He encouraged singing constantly. He understood the value of singing implicitly. He knew that the right music being brought forth in the right way at the right time could literally make miracles happen.

It is for this reason that we turn to his words on

Too Much Drama:
A Biblical Perspective

music for some insight as to how it can enhance or reduce the drama in our lives.

The Points:

Listen to what we can learn from missionary Paul about music.

1. Use the music to encourage other people. (Ephesians 5: 19)

2. Use the music to encourage yourself. (Ephesians 5: 19)

3. Use the music to give thanks. (Ephesians 5: 20)

4. Use the music to get you through the night. (Acts 16: 25)

5. Use the music to worship the Lord. (Colossians 3: 16)

Too Much Drama:
A Biblical Perspective

The Practice:

Here is how you can put this passage into practice.

1. Music is a gift that can calm you down.

2. Music is a gift that can cheer you up.

3. Music is a gift that can carry you through.

The Ponderings:

1. What is your favorite song? Why?

2. How has music been a part of your life?

3. How does music function in your life?

4. Why do you think music plays such a major role in both public and private praise and worship?

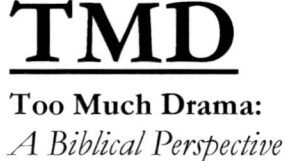

Too Much Drama:
A Biblical Perspective

12.
The Curtain
It Separates You

The Passage: Matthew 27: 45-53

45 Now from the sixth hour until the ninth hour there was darkness over all the land. 46And about the ninth hour Jesus cried out with a loud voice, saying, "Eli, Eli, lama sabachthani?" that is, "My God, My God, why have You forsaken Me?" 47Some of those who stood there, when they heard that, said, "This Man is calling for Elijah!" 48Immediately one of them ran and took a sponge, filled it with sour wine and put it on a reed, and offered it to Him to drink.

49The rest said, "Let Him alone; let us see if Elijah will come to save Him."

50And Jesus cried out again with a loud voice, and yielded up His spirit.

51Then, behold, the veil of the temple was torn in two from top to bottom; and the earth quaked, and the rocks were split, 52and the graves were opened; and many bodies of the saints who had fallen asleep were raised; 53and coming out of the graves after His resurrection, they went into the holy city and appeared to many.

Too Much Drama:
A Biblical Perspective

The Place: The Temple

Jesus was crucified outside of the city of Jerusalem at a place called Calvary. Still, the ramifications and the reverberations of this act were felt a good distance away at the temple in town. According to our text, the veil in the temple was torn in two from top to bottom when Jesus gave up the ghost and died.

The veil in the temple was a curtain inside the holy of holies which separated the holy place from the most holy place. It was here that the Ark of the Covenant rested and where the High Priest entered only once a year to atone for his sins and those of the nation of Israel. Only the High Priest was allowed to enter into this place and even he could only enter once a year.

The significance of the veil being torn in two was that the separation between God and humanity was ended by the sacrificial death of our Lord. Jesus, our new High Priest, had opened the way for those who believe in Him to have direct access to the Father at any time. When this curtain was removed, it ushered in a new act in the drama of the relationship

TMD

Too Much Drama:
A Biblical Perspective

between God and his human creation.

The Points:

What a difference a curtain can make!

1. The veil in the temple was a sign of separation from God. (Ephesians 2: 14-18)

2. When Jesus died, the fact that the veil was torn in two meant that the separation between God and humanity was over. (Ephesians 2: 14)

3. Now, as a result of the death of Jesus, those who believe in Him can:

    a. See into the Holy Place. (Acts 7: 54-56)

    b. Go into the Holy Place. (Ephesians 2: 18)

    c. Stand in the Holy Place. (Romans 14: 10)

    d. Abide in the Holy Place. (John 15: 4-9)

Too Much Drama:
A Biblical Perspective

    e. Become a Holy Place. (I Corinthians 6: 19-20)

The Practice:

Here is how you can put this passage into practice.

1. Now that the curtain has been removed, take advantage of your access to God.

2. Now that the curtain has been removed, do not act as if you have to be separated from God.

3. Now that the curtain has been removed, come boldly before the throne of God.

The Ponderings:

1. What, if anything, do you use as a curtain to hide behind?

2. How can the removal of the separation between God and humanity create anxiety and fear within us?

TMD
Too Much Drama:
A Biblical Perspective

3. How can you take advantage of having open access to God?

4. When the curtain was torn in two, it meant

   that we could go into the presence of God. It also meant that God's presence could come out to us! Elaborate on this.

Too Much Drama:
A Biblical Perspective

13.
The Audience
It Watches You

The Passage: II Samuel 6: 12-23

12Now it was told King David, saying, "The LORD has blessed the house of Obed-Edom and all that belongs to him, because of the ark of God." So David went and brought up the ark of God from the house of Obed-Edom to the City of David with gladness. 13And so it was, when those bearing the ark of the LORD had gone six paces, that he sacrificed oxen and fatted sheep. 14Then David danced before the LORD with all his might; and David was wearing a linen ephod. 15So David and all the house of Israel brought up the ark of the LORD with shouting and with the sound of the trumpet.

16Now as the ark of the LORD came into the City of David, Michal, Saul's daughter, looked through a window and saw King David leaping and whirling before the LORD; and she despised him in her heart. 17So they brought the ark of the LORD, and set it in its place in the midst of the tabernacle that David had erected for it. Then David offered burnt offerings and peace offerings before the LORD. 18And when David had finished offering burnt offerings and peace offerings, he blessed the people in the name of the LORD of hosts. 19Then he distributed among all the people,

TMD

Too Much Drama:
A Biblical Perspective

among the whole multitude of Israel, both the women and the men, to everyone a loaf of bread, a piece of meat, and a cake of raisins. So all the people departed, everyone to his house.

[20]Then David returned to bless his household. And Michal the daughter of Saul came out to meet David, and said, "How glorious was the king of Israel today, uncovering himself today in the eyes of the maids of his servants, as one of the base fellows shamelessly uncovers himself!"

[21]So David said to Michal, "It was before the LORD, who chose me instead of your father and all his house, to appoint me ruler over the people of the LORD, over Israel. Therefore I will play music before the LORD. [22]And I will be even more undignified than this, and will be humble in my own sight. But as for the maidservants of whom you have spoken, by them I will be held in honor."

[23]Therefore Michal the daughter of Saul had no children to the day of her death.

The Person: David

In a former lesson, we watched David step onto the hallowed stage of Hebrew history. There, the focus was on the stage or the actual arena in which he was able to showcase his gifts. Now, what takes our

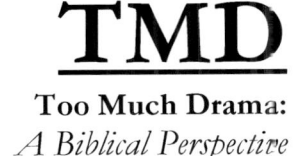

Too Much Drama:
A Biblical Perspective

attention is not the stage on which he stood, but the audience before whom he played.

A study of the various trials, tribulations and triumphs of David will readily reveal that he was always keenly aware of his audience. In fact, as this present passage suggests, he was not at all bashful to do his thing *before the Lord!*

The Points:

Let's review David and some of his various audiences.

1. David acted as a mad man before King Achish. (I Samuel 21: 10-15)

2. David defied and defeated Goliath before all of Israel. (I Samuel 17: 40-47)

3. David played his harp before King Saul. (I Samuel 16: 14-23)

4. David sinned before the Lord. (Psalm 51: 3-4)

Too Much Drama:
A Biblical Perspective

5. David repented before the Lord. (Psalm 51: 1-2)

6. David danced before the Lord. (II Samuel 6: 12-15)

7. David sat before the Lord (II Samuel 7: 18)

The Practice:

Here is how you can put this passage into practice.

1. You are somebody else's audience.

2. Somebody else is your audience.

3. The Lord is watching you, whether or not He is your intended audience.

The Ponderings:

1. Give an example of someone you found out was watching you while you were unaware of it.

Too Much Drama:
A Biblical Perspective

2. How does who you consider to be your audience affect your actions?

3. What does it mean to intentionally have God as your audience?

4. How might your actions change if you thought someone was watching you *all the time?*

TMD
Too Much Drama:
A Biblical Perspective

14.
The Critics
They Focus You

The Passage: Nehemiah 2: 19-20; 4: 1-13

Nehemiah 2: 19-20

19 But when Sanballat the Horonite, Tobiah the Ammonite official, and Geshem the Arab heard of it, they laughed at us and despised us, and said, "What is this thing that you are doing? Will you rebel against the king?"

20 So I answered them, and said to them, "The God of heaven Himself will prosper us; therefore we His servants will arise and build, but you have no heritage or right or memorial in Jerusalem."

Nehemiah 4: 1-13

1 But it so happened, when Sanballat heard that we were rebuilding the wall, that he was furious and very indignant, and mocked the Jews. 2 And he spoke before his brethren and the army of Samaria, and said, "What are these feeble Jews doing? Will they fortify themselves? Will they offer sacrifices? Will they complete it in a day? Will they revive the stones from the heaps of rubbish-- stones that are burned?"

Too Much Drama:
A Biblical Perspective

3Now Tobiah the Ammonite was beside him, and he said, "Whatever they build, if even a fox goes up on it, he will break down their stone wall."

4Hear, O our God, for we are despised; turn their reproach on their own heads, and give them as plunder to a land of captivity! 5Do not cover their iniquity, and do not let their sin be blotted out from before You; for they have provoked You to anger before the builders.

6So we built the wall, and the entire wall was joined together up to half its height, for the people had a mind to work.

7Now it happened, when Sanballat, Tobiah, the Arabs, the Ammonites, and the Ashdodites heard that the walls of Jerusalem were being restored and the gaps were beginning to be closed, that they became very angry, 8and all of them conspired together to come and attack Jerusalem and create confusion. 9Nevertheless we made our prayer to our God, and because of them we set a watch against them day and night.

10Then Judah said, "The strength of the laborers is failing, and there is so much rubbish that we are not able to build the wall." 11And our adversaries said, "They will neither know nor see anything, till we come into their midst and kill them and cause the work to cease."

12So it was, when the Jews who dwelt near them came, that they

TMD

Too Much Drama:
A Biblical Perspective

told us ten times, "From whatever place you turn, they will be upon us." 13Therefore I positioned men behind the lower parts of the wall, at the openings; and I set the people according to their families, with their swords, their spears, and their bows.

The Person: Nehemiah

Like many of his countrymen, Nehemiah was a Jew who lived outside of Israel. Unlike most of his countrymen, he had risen through the ranks to land a high profile, high impact and high powered job in Persia as King Artaxerxes' cup bearer.

As such, he stood next to the king. He regularly sat in the presence of the king. He walked along with the king. He tasted the wine for the king. He advised the king. He was friends with the king. Anyone else would have been satisfied with this set up, but Nehemiah was not.

The matter which brought him misery, as he sat in the splendor of the king's throne room, was that his native city, Jerusalem, was in distress. He could not sleep knowing that the holy city was in shambles, its gates had been burned and its walls were in disrepair.

Too Much Drama:
A Biblical Perspective

One day, the king noticed sadness on Nehemiah's face. When Nehemiah told him why he was sad, the king gave him permission and money to return to Jerusalem to rebuild the walls. When Nehemiah arrived there, instead of being greeted by cheers, he was met with jeers. Instead of having blessings hurled at him, he heard boos shouted at him. Instead of being welcomed with celebration, he came face to face with harsh and cruel criticism.

The example of Nehemiah shows us that criticism is to be expected by anyone who ever attempts to do anything of substance. The key, though, is not to sit around waiting for it to come. Rather, it lies in knowing what to do when it comes and how to overcome it.

The Points:

When it comes to critics:

1. Expect them. (Nehemiah 4: 1-2; 7-8)

2. Talk to God about them. (Nehemiah 4: 4-6)

TMD

Too Much Drama:
A Biblical Perspective

---

3. Answer them. (Nehemiah 6: 3; 8-9)

4. Learn from them. (Nehemiah 4: 7-9)

5. Make necessary adjustments because of them. (Nehemiah 4: 9; 12-13)

6. If you are about a great work, keep going in spite of them. (Nehemiah 6: 3-4)

The Practice:

Here is how you can put this passage into practice.

1. Include criticism as a necessary part of your growth and prosperity.

2. Take criticism like you eat fish. Eat the meat and spit out the bones.

3. Let the critics do their job. You do yours.

Too Much Drama:
A Biblical Perspective

The Ponderings:

1. How can criticism help us stay focused?

2. How can criticism help us grow?

3. How can criticism help us remain motivated?

4. How can criticism help us depend upon God?

Too Much Drama:
A Biblical Perspective

15.
The Applause
It Praises You

The Passage: John 12: 42-43

42 Nevertheless even among the rulers many believed in Him, but because of the Pharisees they did not confess Him, lest they should be put out of the synagogue; 43 for they loved the praise of men more than the praise of God.

The People: The Secret Believers

In the twelfth chapter of the Gospel of John, we read about certain rulers of the Jews who secretly believed in Jesus. They had been among the multitudes which saw His miracles and they were thoroughly convinced that He was the Messiah.

The only problem was that unlike the crowd on the first Palm Sunday, they refused to come out into the open with their commitment to and praise for the Lord. The reason the Bible gives for this is that a policy had been established that anyone who believed in Jesus would be put out of the synagogue.

Too Much Drama:
A Biblical Perspective

Hence, these rulers kept their convictions secret because *they loved the praise of men more than God.*

What a sorry state of affairs it must be when religious rulers prefer the applause of people over the applause of God. Unfortunately, we cannot afford to shake our heads or fists in disgust at that generation because as it was then, so it is now.

The Points:

What we know about these rulers who secretly believed:

1. They loved their positions. (John 12: 42)

2. They loved their religious and social asscciations. (John 12: 42)

3. They loved the praise of men. (John 12: 43)

4. They loved the praise of men more than the praise of God. (John 12: 43)

TMD

Too Much Drama:
A Biblical Perspective

The Practice:

Here is how you can put this passage into practice.

1. The person whose applause you seek will influence your behavior.

2. The applause you receive is contingent upon your satisfying the one who applauds.

3. The applause you receive will not last forever.

4. The applause of God comes as we obey and worship Him.

The Ponderings:

1. Whose applause do you seek?

2. What has been the price of that applause?

3. Who do you applaud? Why?

4. What is it that we can do to make God applaud us?

Too Much Drama:
A Biblical Perspective

16.
The Drama
It Blesses You

The Passage: Genesis 50: 15-21

15 When Joseph's brothers saw that their father was dead, they said, "Perhaps Joseph will hate us, and may actually repay us for all the evil which we did to him." 16So they sent messengers to Joseph, saying, "Before your father died he commanded, saying, 17"Thus you shall say to Joseph: "I beg you, please forgive the trespass of your brothers and their sin; for they did evil to you."' Now, please, forgive the trespass of the servants of the God of your father." And Joseph wept when they spoke to him.

18Then his brothers also went and fell down before his face, and they said, "Behold, we are your servants."

19Joseph said to them, "Do not be afraid, for am I in the place of God? 20But as for you, you meant evil against me; but God meant it for good, in order to bring it about as it is this day, to save many people alive. 21Now therefore, do not be afraid; I will provide for you and your little ones." And he comforted them and spoke kindly to them.

Too Much Drama:
A Biblical Perspective

The Person: Joseph

The last thirteen chapters of the *Book of Genesis* recount the drama of Jacob's beloved son Joseph. It is here that we read about his dreams and his coat of many colors. It is in this last part of Genesis that we hear about the jealousy of his brothers and their plot, first to kill him and then to sell him into slavery.

It is in this section of the Bible that we find out about the "wilds of Potiphar's wife" and Joseph's perils in prison. It is in this part of the Holy Scripture that he ascends to be the Prime Minister of Egypt, second only to Pharaoh.

At the place where we enter his story now, his father, Jacob, had just died and his brothers feared that Joseph would retaliate against them for what they did to him in his youth. Much to their surprise, his brothers find him gracious instead of grumbling. They find him to be reflective instead of wrathful. They find him joyful instead of spiteful.

Apparently, through it all, Joseph had arrived at the point where he could embrace his drama as the necessary journey which led him to his destiny.

Too Much Drama:
A Biblical Perspective

When we can look at our drama this way, somehow it does not seem so bad!

The Points:

At the end of the drama, Joseph was not bitter. In fact, he was gracious and humble because:

1. He survived the drama. (Genesis 45: 25-28)

2. He wept about the drama. (Genesis 50: 17)

3. He realized the role of the other characters in the drama. (Genesis 50: 20)

4. He understood the purpose of the drama. (Genesis 50: 20)

5. He was able to be a blessing because of the drama. (Genesis 50: 21)

The Practice:

Here is how you can put this passage into practice.

TMD

Too Much Drama:
A Biblical Perspective

1. *End*ure your drama. (Make it to the end.)

2. Embrace your drama.

3. Enjoy your drama.

The Ponderings:

1. What is it that keeps us going through our drama all the way to the end?

2. Have you ever been able to look back and see the positive purpose of what was, at the time, a major drama? Explain.

3. Have you ever had adversaries who moved you to a better place in life in spite of their efforts to hinder and hurt you? Elaborate.

4. Can you see the hand of God active in the drama of your life?

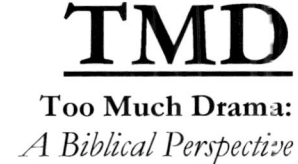
Too Much Drama:
A Biblical Perspective

17.
The Credits
They Helped You

The Passage: Psalm 107: 1-31

1 Oh, give thanks to the LORD, for He is good! For His mercy endures forever. 2Let the redeemed of the LORD say so, Whom He has redeemed from the hand of the enemy, 3And gathered out of the lands, From the east and from the west, From the north and from the south.

4They wandered in the wilderness in a desolate way; They found no city to dwell in. 5Hungry and thirsty, Their soul fainted in them. 6Then they cried out to the LORD in their trouble, And He delivered them out of their distresses. 7And He led them forth by the right way, That they might go to a city for a dwelling place. 8Oh, that men would give thanks to the LORD for His goodness, And for His wonderful works to the children of men!

9For He satisfies the longing soul, And fills the hungry soul with goodness. 10Those who sat in darkness and in the shadow of death, Bound in affliction and irons-- 11Because they rebelled against the words of God, And despised the counsel of the Most High, 12Therefore He brought down their heart with labor; They fell down, and there was none to help. 13Then they cried out to the

TMD
Too Much Drama:
A Biblical Perspective

LORD in their trouble, And He saved them out of their distresses. 14He brought them out of darkness and the shadow of death, And broke their chains in pieces. 15Oh, that men would give thanks to the LORD for His goodness, And for His wonderful works to the children of men! 16For He has broken the gates of bronze, And cut the bars of iron in two.

17Fools, because of their transgression, And because of their iniquities, were afflicted. 18Their soul abhorred all manner of food, And they drew near to the gates of death. 19Then they cried out to the LORD in their trouble, And He saved them out of their distresses. 20He sent His word and healed them, And delivered them from their destructions. 21Oh, that men would give thanks to the LORD for His goodness, And for His wonderful works to the children of men! 22Let them sacrifice the sacrifices of thanksgiving, And declare His works with rejoicing. 23Those who go down to the sea in ships, Who do business on great waters, 24They see the works of the LORD, And His wonders in the deep. 25For He commands and raises the stormy wind, Which lifts up the waves of the sea. 26They mount up to the heavens, They go down again to the depths; Their soul melts because of trouble. 27They reel to and fro, and stagger like a drunken man, And are at their wits' end. 28Then they cry out to the LORD in their trouble, And He brings them out of their distresses. 29He calms the storm, So that its waves are still.

30Then they are glad because they are quiet; So He guides them to their desired haven. 31Oh, that men would give thanks to the LORD for His goodness, And for His wonderful works to the

Too Much Drama:
A Biblical Perspective

children of men!

The Person: The Psalmist

We may not know exactly who this psalmist is, but we do know exactly what he said about giving God the credit for the victories in our lives. Too often, as soon as a movie is over, we start to put on our coats, try to rush out ahead of the crowd and never pay attention to the names in fine print flying across the screen.

These are the people who put the movie together. These are the people whose faces you never see. These are the people who make the stars shine. These are the people who do the grunt work. These are the people who bring the movie to the screen. These are the people who deserve the credit.

What this psalmist is doing is asking us to pause just a minute to review the acts of God in our drama. When we do, we will have to give Him the credit and the praise.

TMD

Too Much Drama:
A Biblical Perspective

The Points:

At the end of a movie, the credits roll by so quickly that we hardly have the time or ability to read them. Here, however, let us slow down and read each credit carefully.

The credit goes to God because:

1. He is good. (Psalm 107: 1)

2. He redeemed us. (Psalm 107: 2)

3. He gathered us. (Psalm 107: 3)

4. He delivered us. (Psalm 107: 6)

5. He led us. (Psalm 107: 7)

6. He satisfies us. (Psalm 107: 9)

7. He saved us. (Psalm 107: 13)

8. He brought us out of darkness. (Psalm 107: 14)

TMD

Too Much Drama:
A Biblical Perspective

9. He healed us. (Psalm 107: 20)

10. He calmed the storm for us. (Psalm 107: 29)

11. He guided us. (Psalm 107: 30)

12. He made us glad. (Psalm 107: 30)

The Practice:

Here is how you can put this passage into practice.

1. The credit goes to the people who work behind the scenes.

2. The credit goes to the people who make the sacrifices.

3. The credit goes to the Lord who is sovereign over everything.

TMD

Too Much Drama:
A Biblical Perspective

The Ponderings:

1. Who are some of the people in your life who deserve the credit for your successes?

2. How have you expressed your appreciation to these people who deserve so much credit?

3. What has the Lord done for you that causes you to want to give Him the credit?

Too Much Drama:
A Biblical Perspective

Don't Have Enough of Too Much Drama?

Too Much Drama: A Biblical Perspective is part of a complete set of materials written by Dr. C. Dexter Wise III to help you identify and deal with all the drama in your life.

Be sure to also get a copy of the **Video** to accompany the notes in this present work and the **full length book**, *Too Much Drama: What to Do When Your Life is Going over the Top.*

Dr. Wise also has a **series of sermons** based on this theme.

For more tapes, books, videos and other resources by Dr. Wise visit www.wiseworksonline.com or write:

Wise Works, Inc.
P.O. Box 0771
Westerville, OH 43086
(614) 898-1997

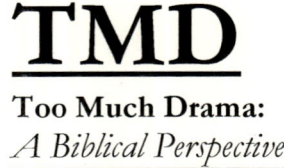
Too Much Drama:
A Biblical Perspective

To study with Dr. Wise in
The Wise School of Ministry
either live, online or on tape visit:

www.thewiseschool.com

To see and hear Dr. Wise preach and teach
anytime of day or night on
Faith Ministries Church's
website visit:

www.FMCTV.com

To be a part of
The International Fellowship of Faith Ministries
visit:

www.iffmus.com